Bailey's Sprouts

With Cabana Nana

Linda Ann Arslanian

Copyright © 2025 by
Linda Ann Arslanian

ALL RIGHTS RESERVED. No part of this book may be reproduced or transmitted in any form by any means, electronic or mechanical, including photocopying and recording, or by any information storage and retrieval system, except as may be expressly permitted in writing from the author.

ISBN: Number

Published by: AMZN Publishers
Company Website: amznpublishers.com

Printed in the United States of America

Dedication

As I sit down to write this dedication, I am forever grateful to my family, some who have passed on and some who are still with me. Their love has made me a strong person who is very happy to appreciate everything in life.

And to my friends, and my partner of many years, Manny, with whom I continue to enjoy and appreciate life together. Love you!

This book is about my granddaughter, Bailey—a ten-year-old.

Acknowledgment

This children's book has been a dream of mine for as long as I can remember and has been on my bucket list for years. Completing this project has been a truly fulfilling journey, and I am so proud to see it finally come to life. Writing this book has allowed me to bring cherished memories and ideas to the page, and it has been a labor of love every step of the way.

I have never been particularly fond of working on computers, but my son, Todd, has always been my biggest cheerleader. He often tells me, "You can do anything, Mom!" That encouragement gave me the confidence to keep going, even when the process felt overwhelming. His words remind me that no matter your age or experience, your dreams are always worth pursuing. To anyone reading this, young or old, I hope my journey inspires you to make your own dreams or thoughts a reality.

A heartfelt thank you goes out to my incredible AMZ book publishing team and our dedicated coordinator, Ron Walker. Your support and expertise have been invaluable. I'm thrilled to see this children's book ready to touch the lives of many readers. My greatest hope is that children and adults alike will enjoy these stories as much as we have. Writing about Ace and Bailey's adventures has brought me immense joy, and I believe their story will bring smiles to many faces.

I will always be grateful for my wonderful family—my sons, Todd and Craig; my daughter-in-law, KA; my grandchildren, Bailey and Ace; my brothers and sisters; my sweethearts and partners, Manny and friends. Your love and encouragement have been my strength.

With all my love,

Mom – Nana – Linda

About the Author

A little about myself. I have worn many hats throughout my life, each one adding a unique chapter to my journey. From being a hairdresser and wig manager to an apartment manager and food school manager, my career has been anything but ordinary. I have also worked as a dental assistant and managed my own restaurant. At one point, I owned a holiday photo company where I created memorable experiences with Santa Claus and the Easter Bunny. Beyond that, I've been a caregiver and even dabbled in the entertainment industry as a movie producer and actress, starring in a film and a music video.

I've embraced thrills and adventures that some can only dream of, including skydiving, parasailing, paragliding, and ziplining. One of my most memorable surprises came from my son, Todd, who arranged a meet and greet with my favorite jazz musician, Kenny G, for my big birthday. Hearing him play his saxophone and serenade me with "Happy Birthday" was a moment I will cherish forever.

I've also enjoyed time on the water, like the unforgettable day I caught a massive fish in the Florida Keys aboard a relative's (Witt) large boat. My love for exploration has taken me to incredible places around the globe, including Spain, Mexico, China, France, and many other countries.

Of all my experiences, the most rewarding has been raising my two amazing sons, my granddaughter, and my grandson. They have filled my life with love, joy, and pride.

As I finalize this book, I feel an immense sense of accomplishment. My bucket list is complete, and my heart is full of gratitude.

Thank you to everyone who has been part of my life's journey.

Cabana Nana,
Linda Ann Arslanian

Table of Contents

Day 1 11

Day 2 16

Day 3 18

Day 4 22

Day 1

Hello,

I am Bailey. I am ten years old. My hobbies are playing video games, mixing and making different colors of slime, drawing, making small crafts and collecting plushies and stuffed animals.

Today is a special day. Cabana Nana called me on her telephone and said, "Bailey, you're ten years old now. How would you like to have your first job?"

"I would love to have a job. But where will I work, Cabana Nana?" I asked her.

"Why, come over and take care of my garden. I could really use the help," she answered.

"Sure!" I said happily. She told me I would have to come over every day and check if her fruits and vegetables needed watering or picking. I was excited as I wanted to make my Cabana Nana proud of me. She had trusted me to do this job well.

I looked at the time. It was 3 o'clock. I prepared myself to go to Cabana Nana's house. I had just gotten home from school, and we had no homework today, so I could spend the afternoon in Cabana Nana's garden. I couldn't wait to see how big her garden was.

Cabana Nana's house was only a few houses over, so it was close enough for me to walk.

When I arrived, I saw a bench outside the garden that was shaped like a bear. I sat down on it and looked at the garden. I couldn't believe how big it was. There were vegetables of all kinds, from fresh green cucumbers to different colored bell peppers and green cabbages. There were also different fruits, such as purple berries and bright red tomatoes.

As I sat there, taking this view in, I smelled something funny. I remember my Cabana Nana once told me that she put vinegar in her garden to get rid of pests and keep the animals out.

I suddenly heard some noise and turned around to see my friends coming towards me. My mom must have told them where I was. They came close and asked me if I wanted to go play video games with them. I politely refused as I had a job to do. I told them I had promised Cabana Nana that I would come help her out in her garden every day.

As we were talking, a beautiful brown, orange, and yellow butterfly fluttered by.

"Did you guys know that an adult butterfly only lives for two weeks? My dad told me this, so we should feel lucky to see this one," I told them.

"Wow!" replied my friends. "Well, I guess if you're not coming, we'll go play our video games. Sorry you can't join us, though." With that, they left.

I was a little sad when I saw my friends leaving. I thought about how I was going to miss out on the video games, but this was my job, and I had to take it seriously.

"There you are, Bailey," came Cabana Nana's voice from behind me. I turned around and saw her wearing her gardening gloves and holding a pair of shears.

"Good afternoon, Cabana Nana. I am here for my job," I replied, getting off the bear seat.

"Good afternoon to you as well. Come, walk with me. We have much to talk about," she replied as she started walking inside the garden.

I quickly followed her steps and as we walked, she told me everything about her garden, watering but making sure the soil isn't overwatered, how to pick the produce and how to keep the pests away. With these instructions, she turned around and left me to take care of her garden.

As I looked around in the garden, I noticed it seemed a little dry. I glanced around and spotted a green hose nearby. I picked the hose up and turned the faucet on. I didn't know that the hose had a hole in it, and as soon as I turned the faucet on, the water sprayed my pants. It seemed silly as if I had accidentally wet my pants. I couldn't help but laugh. Thank goodness, no one was there to see it.

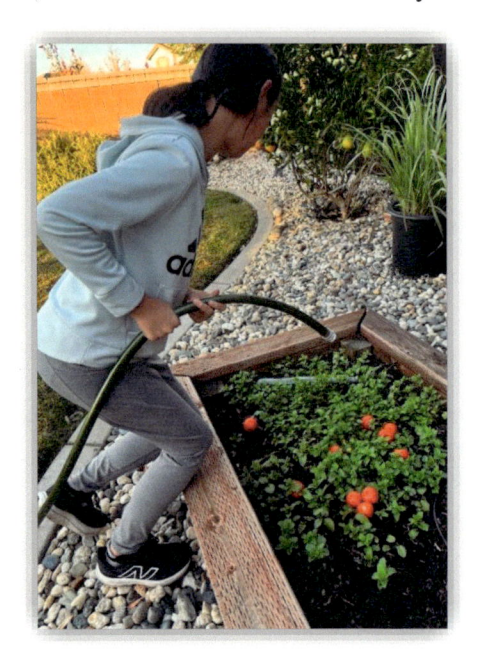

Hooray! I did it. I remembered not to overwater the soil as I remembered Cabana Nana had told me it was not good to do.

I looked at the tomatoes and saw that some of them weren't firm and red. They can't have one side green as they won't be ready to pick then.

I then noticed it was getting a little dark, so I decided to walk home and come back tomorrow. I got back home, and my mother was busy with my little brother, Ace.

"How is Cabana Nana?" asked my dad.

I excitedly told him she had given me a job to look after her garden.

"Wow, Bailey," he exclaimed. "Cabana Nana must really trust you, as she loves her garden."

We had dinner, and then I went to sleep. As I fell asleep, I had a dream. In my dream, I saw many strawberries, tomatoes, and cucumbers. There were bananas that had thirty-foot stems. Suddenly, there was a strong, windy storm. These banana stems were so strong that despite the strong winds, they stayed put.

Day 2

The next day, when I woke up, I felt happy that the storm was just in my dream. There was no storm outside.

It was Saturday today, and we had no school. I brushed my teeth, dressed up, had my breakfast cereal, and told my mother that I was going to Cabana Nana's house. When I arrived, Cabana Nana said, "Good morning, Bailey! I am so happy to see you are taking care of my garden. I noticed you watered the garden yesterday. You're doing a great job."

"Thank you, Cabana Nana," I replied. "But I should tell you, there is a hole in your hose."

"Okay, I will buy a new one," she said. I told her how I had water all over my pants because of the hole in the hose, and it made it look like I had wet my pants. We both laughed.

Cabana Nana told me that her veggies were doing good, getting at least six to ten hours of direct sunlight per day.

"With our good soil, we should be getting a lot of veggies and fruit as long as the weather stays good," she told me.

As we walked through her garden, I told her about the dream and the bad storm.

"Oh, I am glad it was just a dream," she said.

It was time for me to go out and see the garden. I looked around and spotted some worms. Cabana Nana told me they came out and went back into the soil. I wasn't worried about them. The soil looked moist and all seemed good to me, so saying goodbye to Cabana Nana, I left for home.

Day 3

Soon, it was the next day. I got up, dressed fast, gulped down my breakfast, and hurried out. My parents asked me where I was going in such a hurry.

"Cabana Nana told me it's been sixty days since she planted strawberries, and they should be ready to pick now," I replied as I slid out the door.

I rushed over to Cabana Nana's house and entered the garden. I was surprised to see a lot of fresh, red strawberries. As we walked together in the patch, Cabana Nana told me that when she first started planting strawberries, only a few plants would produce around thirty or so pounds of strawberries per season. She also told me homegrown berries were sweeter and healthier as she never used any chemicals in her garden.

She then left to go to the store. I was hungry, so I picked up an apple that had fallen on the ground. I bit into it. *'Oh no!'* I thought to myself as I spotted a worm inside.

'Next time, I will look at it and wash my apple before I take a bite.'

I noticed a few large open containers nearby. I was so excited I thought I would surprise my Nana and pick the strawberries myself. This took some time, and I was very careful as I wanted to do a good job.

I finally finished, so I went inside Cabana Nana's house and put the strawberry filled large containers on the table. Nana was still at the store, so I left the house and came back home. I was tired after all the hard work. I kept thinking how hard farmers and horticulturists must work.

Later that night, Cabana Nana telephoned my parents.

"Ka, can you and my son Craig come over? Please bring Bailey and Ace as well," she said.

"Sure, we will come over right after dinner," replied my mom. We had Aunt Debbie, Aunt Clara, Uncle Todd, Uncle Jerry, Uncle James, Uncle Kenny, Manny, and some friends.

After dinner, when all the company left, Mom said we could go visit Cabana Nana. As Mom, Dad, Ace and I made our way toward Cabana Nana's house, we saw her standing at the front door with a big smile on her face.

"Come inside. Look at all the work Bailey did today," she said.

Cabana Nana had put the strawberries in baskets for us to take home.

"I am so proud of you, Bailey. You worked so hard filling up these big containers with strawberries. I was so surprised when I came back from the store," she smiled.

I then reached over and gave my brother a big, fat strawberry. He smiled wide. My mom, dad, and Cabana Nana made me feel so proud of myself. I learned that night that this feeling was better than wasting my time playing. I will never forget my first job and that big garden. Cabana Nana said that I had learned a good lesson and that many more lessons to learn were awaiting me.

Soon, my mom told us it was time for us to get back home as it was getting late. We carried the baskets of strawberries back home.

When we got home, my dad called me in the living room.

"Bailey, I cannot begin to tell you how proud you have made me, taking on the job of Nana's garden, and on top of that, Ace told me that instead of going out and wasting time playing video games, my sister has leveled up and continued her duty taking care of that garden. So you see, Bailey, you have taught Ace a great lesson at his age. I am proud of you," he said.

I was so happy that I couldn't stop smiling after that. It was bedtime soon, and I felt happy but really tired. I wanted to stay up late, thinking about my accomplishment, but I had school the next day, and not sleeping on time is a bad idea on a school night. You end up sleeping in class the next day. It is best to be well rested so you don't end up sleeping and actually learn your lessons in class.

Day 4

The next day, after school, Cabana Nana was picking up Ace and me to go to Manny's house to visit the chickens in his backyard. He had a chicken coup, and we were to collect fresh eggs for my mom to bake. As we entered the coup, one of the chickens flew close to Ace's face, and he stepped back. We both laughed and began collecting the eggs carefully. We left with around 18 eggs.

"Good, you collected fresh eggs to bring home," said Manny as we entered his house. Cabana Nana told him to tell Ace and me what happened to that pesty squirrel that had been eating Manny's garden for some time now.

"Well, it had been eating my garden for a few years now, and I got tired of it, so I decided to set up a trap and catch him. I put the trap near the garden and put a big pile of nuts inside. Guess what! The next day, that squirrel was inside the trap."

"So what did you do with the squirrel then?" I asked.

"I sprayed its tail with a red, non-toxic paint," he replied.

"Why?" I asked again, confused.

"Why, so that I can recognize it if it comes back to attack my garden," he laughed. Cabana Nana was also laughing along.

Soon, Manny told us that we were going for a ride in the park. As we settled in his car, I heard a noise. I looked behind and saw a metal cage with a squirrel inside. The squirrel had a red tail.

"We're going to drop him off far away so he doesn't come back. If he does, I will know it is him by his tail."

When we reached the park, Manny opened the trap, and that squirrel ran away. Maybe it learned a lesson that he had picked the wrong garden too many times.

Not only did Bailey learn a good lesson about gardening with Cabana Nana that week, but maybe the pesty squirrel also learned a lesson that you don't keep destroying someone's garden.

25

Made in the USA
Columbia, SC
04 April 2025